Living in a Dream

Bluff Country Offerings

by Nancy Overcott

Illustrations by Dana Gardner

Preface to the Lost Lake Folk Art Premier Edition
by Tom Driscoll

SHIPWRECKT BOOKS PUBLISHING COMPANY
Raising independent publishing to the level of indie music & film

Lost Lake Folk Art
PO Box 20
Lanesboro, MN 55949

IN®
DIE

Cover Design by Shipwreckt Books

Cover Drawing by Dana Gardner

Winter's Last

Preface to Lost Lake Folk Art Premier Edition, *Living in a Dream*

Never will I forget my Border Collie Brother, when just young, how he patrolled back of the house, the rising bluff there shaggy with chipmunks and squirrels. Suddenly, as if a silent signal beeped in his head, he would bolt around-front to the retaining wall and my wife's street-side garden, all hand-painted-summer with tall prairie grasses and drooping irises. More often than not, Brother scared-up a feast of dunny birds munching the plump fruit off gangly red osiers and service berry bushes, triggering a starburst of feathers.

Old now, so slowed he seems to barely move most days, Brother still keeps crocodilian watch over the birds in his yard, living simultaneously in-the-moment with sparrows and cardinals queued up at snowy feeders, and deep in his personal past, intimate memories of herding out of spring into winter a lifetime of fascinating, colorful birds.

Readers familiar with past collaborations by essayist Nancy Overcott and illustrator Dana Gardner will likely remember all the fascinating, colorful birds the two naturalists have given substance and context in generous, beautiful books entitled with palpable Upper Midwestern dryness: *Fifty Common Birds of the Upper Midwest*, and its mirror tessellation, *Fifty Uncommon Birds of the Upper Midwest* (University of Iowa Press, 2006-2007), and an earlier volume, *At Home in the Big Woods* (Taxon Media, 2002).

Open the front cover of *Fifty Common Birds* – its dust jacket is sumptuously decorated with a veritable wooden model of red-eyed perfection, Mr. Gardner's watercolor rendering of the once locally endangered wood duck floating serenely over its own reflection out from behind a low-dangling elm branch – the index of deeply personal essays by Ms. Overcott, a retired nurse, reads like a poem, or a folk ditty: eastern kingbird, red-eyed vireo, **b**lue jay, tree swallow, barn swallow, black-capped chickadee.

Though my own birding skills are pedestrian at best, I am, like my old dog Brother, an unapologetic bird lover, an aficionado of the tangle of morning songs, mating calls and puffed-up threats tumbling from woods and thickets; a fan of odd-sounding names, admirer of feathers and beaks and sleek bird bodies in flight. But I had never before observed birders until, in June 2006, as a prelude to reviewing *Fifty Common Birds*, I accompanied Nancy and Dana on a birding hike through summer prairie to a precipitous overlook of the Root River near Pilot Mound in Southeast Minnesota. I remember, at one point Nancy stopped, touched fingers to her ear as if to unstitch the tapestry of birds, insects and wanton woodland noises. She said, "I'm hearing a yellow-billed cuckoo." Immediately, all idle talk ceased while she and Dana scanned a nearby corner of timber with their binoculars until they spotted their bird. Isolating birds by sound, glimpsing a tuft of color out of the corner of the eye, making the ID, zooming in for a closer look, I learned from the author and illustrator, that's all a part of birding.

In *Living in a Dream, Bluff Country Offerings*, the esteemed premier edition of Lost Lake Folk Art – though perhaps Maiden Voyage is more an apt analogy for one of Shipwreckt Books Publishing Company's three imprints – Nancy and Dana have teamed-up once again to watch over the birds, as it were, to simultaneously create new works in-the-moment and reflect on the past, on their memories. The result is a study in counterpoint: Nancy's always lucid prose searching the dark, tangled timber for a spot of intense color, Dana's sharp, black-ink illustrations leaving the imagination to paint its own image on pure white backdrops.

Many of Nancy's essays look out at the world from one of the porches or windows of the house she and her husband Art built on sixty-two acres in the Big Woods near Canton, Minnesota thirty-six years ago. That hand-crafted house may well be gone now. Nancy and Art sold their land to the DNR in 2008 and the acreage is now a wildlife area. Nancy and Art moved to the small city of Preston, Fillmore County seat, forty-five miles south of Rochester.

It's the overlap of past and present, life in the Big Woods and small town life, that is the canvas, the backdrop for *Living in a Dream*.

Dana Gardner was born in Wisconsin and moved to Lanesboro when he was seven. Lanesboro is where he admittedly developed a graphic nostalgia for the similar fields and woods, favorite paths, farm ponds, river banks, overlooks and porches that figure intimately in Nancy's articulate prose. A professional illustrator and freelance artist, Dana has lived in Berkeley, California for more than a decade.

Nancy's writing is deeply personal, spilling emotion over into the otherwise common, sometimes unduly harsh, sometimes overly-sentimental natural world. Her essays and Dana's drawings work together as a contrapuntal sonata, two independent melodies meshing beautifully: Dana's impeccable representation of birds on the wing, others nesting, rodents, insects and flowers, everything seeming to stare back into the lens, and Nancy's informative essays, full of facts above all, but laced with mundane observation, personal philosophy and physical, hands-on interaction between the birder and the birds, the side porch, memories of the Big Woods and reflections on town living, a veritable dream world trapped in memory.

Living in a Dream is an uncommon book in an all too common world, one that offers something tactile, sensory for practically everyone of any age. Young eyes and old eyes alike can wander through Dana's stunning illustrations, at once educational and flat-out pleasing to look at, then read Nancy's well-crafted prose, unpretentious, subtly rewarding to anyone willing to enter the dream with her.

It is both fitting and a great honor to introduce Lost Lake Folk Art with this premier volume, *Living in a Dream* by Nancy Overcott and Dana Gardner. It sets the tone perfectly for all books to come. Lost Lake Folk Art is a small Shipwreckt Books imprint committed to publishing any author with a story to tell, anyone with a memory worth capturing forever in print or electronically, an heirloom for future readers.

Tom Driscoll, Managing Editor & CEO

SHIPWRECKT BOOKS PUBLISHING COMPANY
Lost Lake Folk Art

Essays

Deer Mouse

Drawings

In Memory of Reuben Blagsvedt

While Sitting on My Porch in January Fog

Today in January fog I see from the corner of my porch, no snow but brown leaves that match the color of my house, hay-colored grass with a tinge of green brighter than it might be without this wetness and the rain gauge post that stands like a sentinel near bird feeders, where woodpeckers, titmice and nuthatches gather peanut butter and suet. I see the woodshed we built in 1978, a rusty propane tank, the silver metal roof of our workshop, a black spruce we planted in 1984 that rises thirty feet in a perfect cone and the poplars that have housed four species of woodpecker nestlings. Behind me through the house and out the kitchen window past winter-colored goldfinch eating sunflower seeds are three giant oaks that guard the yellow cabin we built in spring 1972.

Straight ahead is the path I have worn while carrying water to the birdbath on the edge of the deep woods where the earth begins to curve down like a globe. The gray sky appears in patches behind bare brown branches of black cherry trees, whose scalloped bark reveals their identities. The hollow log where an opossum once lived is disappearing into the soil.

A gray squirrel travels its traditional path through the trees, then on the ground to the feeders for dropped seeds. A blue jay screeches and a chickadee sings its spring song. An airplane drones. A puff of wind stirs my wind chime. A neighbor's gunshot pierces the air as do the sounds of a pileated woodpecker, who vigorously flies through the woods, flashing its flaming red crest and white wing patches, before attaching itself to a barkless elm and sending wood chips flying with its great bill.

Flying Pileated Woodpecker

In spite of the intention to notice all that surrounds me, my mind wanders to a summer on this porch when I wondered if it takes others as long as I to read a poem, allowing time to let surroundings mesh with the words. In "The Steeple-Jack," Marianne Moore wrote about a sea that changed color by its nature as Dürer changed the color of the Tyrol Mountains with his painting, thus teaching me about juxtapositions of natural and human artifacts and how to see the deep woods from the edge of this porch.

Another summer, I read the poems of Jorie Graham in early mornings while looking up to see the trees taking shape. As I entered the mornings, I became larger and less discrete. In "Relativity: a Quartet," Graham wrote about wanting to get inside a leaf, to experience all its attributes, its cells, chambers and photosynthetic tissue. I studied a green leaf, traced its veins and thought of my own, watched it slowly turn brown and brittle until finally it frightened me. I entered the shadow of a branch and heard a single note so soft it could have been my breath.

My mind wanders to a time before this porch, the summer of 1971, when my husband Art and I were driving back to Minneapolis from a year in Arizona. During that drive, we decided to join the 1970s march of idealistic young adults in the back-to-the-land movement. We planned to buy some property, build our own house and become self-sufficient.

And now I sit here remembering the January day in 1972 when we discovered this piece of land in the blufflands of southeast Minnesota where white snow against black branches made us see in a different way as we listened to the South Fork of the Root River, a spring fed stream, snaking through the valley below this house that we built in 1977 with our own four hands.

The old man who appeared like a mirage out of the woods just as we began our little cabin, our first building on this land, has appeared to me many times over the years, although he is long since dead. Reuben Blagsvedt, our closest neighbor, lived in an old ramshackle house attached to an even older log house down by the South Fork. He said he was curious about the hammering he heard in the woods. "Who are you, then?" he asked. We gave him our names and told him our plans. He was friendly, but we could see he wasn't sure what to make of us, although he did invite us to visit him anytime we wished.

3

On my first visit to Reuben, I saw sheep grazing in the yard and a dead dog still chained to its doghouse. Standing in the doorway of the house was another man, tall and loose limbed with a long scraggly beard and a shotgun over his shoulder. "Paid too much for that rough land," said Reuben's son Leland, better known as Pancake. Reuben slowly stood up from a dilapidated wooden chair and invited me in. Garner Ted Armstrong was speaking over a battery-operated radio. Wasps were flying from a huge nest in and out of the house.

Reuben thanked me for the homemade bread I brought him and carefully placed it in a kitchen drawer. He dipped a coffeepot into a barrel of water and placed it on a wood stove. Soon he offered me coffee and Oreo cookies. The three of us sat around the table talking about religion, social justice and life in the Big Woods. When I rose to leave, the old man said I should walk back to our property along the township road; it might not be safe walking through the woods.

From then on, whenever we visited our land, I visited Reuben and Pancake. By fall, our cabin was complete and we no longer had to sleep in our car. One evening as we were finishing dinner, two mules pulling a covered wagon came up our driveway and we met our neighbors Phyllis and Bobby Norby for the first time. On a ride in their wagon down the old tractor path to the South Fork, we learned that Reuben's wife Lydia had frozen to death under an old maple on our land just before we bought it. Lydia was easily confused and had gone looking for ice cream at the country store in the settlement of Amherst and had lost her way. I suppose that's why Reuben had warned me about walking through the woods.

The Norbys, along with people in the little town of Mabel, told us something about the history of this Big Woods. The land mostly consists of small parcels from which area farmers once cut wood for heating, cooking and building. From the 1920s into the 1960s many squatters, with the implied acquiescence of the farmers, lived here in tarpaper shacks or travel trailers. To support themselves, they fished, hunted, grew

4

vegetables and worked for local lumbermen. The community was closely knit and inhabitants watched out for each other. Moonshine stills were common. And outlaws found the woods a good place to hide from the local sheriff. This hillbilly like culture frightened the good people of neighboring towns, some of whom to this day avoid the woods.

Amherst Store

Six years passed before we permanently moved to our land from Minneapolis. During this time, the Big Woods was our refuge. Whenever we visited it, in addition to spending time with Reuben and Pancake, I took long walks and put my arms around trees, promising to return. I was aware of birds surrounding me but didn't try to name them. The wildflowers were glorious, but I couldn't name most of them either. We met more of our neighbors, including Melvin, an elderly Norwegian bachelor farmer who lived with his cocker spaniel in a mobile home near the entrance to our driveway. Ted Thompson, another old Norwegian bachelor farmer, who lived at the end of the road past Norby's, often stopped to check on Melvin. Merlin Vickerman and his sons frequently patrolled the road past our property in their old pickup truck.

On our first trip to the country store in Amherst, we met Lily Haagenson, proprietor of the store, a wizened woman who looked older than her sixty some years. She spoke to us in a loud voice, "Are you the people who bought that land over there in the Big Woods? I wouldn't want to live there. Too lonely for me." Lily had grown up in the woods and Amherst was on its edge.

The store, an unpainted wood frame building that once housed a creamery, wasn't recognizable as a store except for a Wonder Bread sign on the door and a gas pump out front. Inside we found shelves holding cigarettes, bread, potato chips and dusty canned goods; a glass case holding whole milk, bologna and locally produced Spring Grove soda; a freezer full of ice cream; and five men in overalls with seed caps on their heads, sitting around a large kerosene heater. One of the men, who we had never met, said, "Heard you went in the ditch with that new Chevy pickup. You've got to get a culvert there on your land. Township has to put it in for you." When we took our two loaves of bread to Lily, she said we could have only one because she had to save some for other customers. When we asked for gas, she only gave us five gallons because she had to save some for the farmers.

During our frequent visits to the store, Lily caught us up on local gossip about people we didn't know, including Mary Lewis and Phil Rutter, who had recently moved to the area from Minneapolis. We were curious about the couple who, like us, had left the city for the Big Woods. We found them in the log cabin they had built at the end of a driveway longer than ours amidst woods, fields and several gardens. Their plan was to live as simply as possible, without electricity or running water. For their intended tree farm, they had already begun planting hybrid American chestnuts. They seemed comfortable with their decision to leave the world of academia for life in the woods. Mary quickly became one of my dearest friends.

Sometimes we had company in our small cabin, friends from the City, my parents, or Art's siblings with their families. Our most frequent visitors were Art's sister, Susie, her husband, Dave, and their two young children, Paula and David. They liked the woods so much they thought about looking for their own property in the area. Our cabin was crowded with the six of us, but we managed and had fun exploring the woods together, picking wildflowers and blackcap raspberries, fishing for trout in the South Fork and finding openings in the limestone bluffs where David was sure Native Americans had lived.

In mid October 1976, two years before we moved to our land, Bobby and Phyllis Norby came to see us in our cabin with sad news. Reuben was in the Spring Grove hospital with cancer. On the night of October 5, Pancake had gone to see his dad, but the nurses wouldn't let him in because he was drunk. Pancake angrily left the hospital, climbed into his truck and sped down the highway right into the path of another car, killing not only himself but the other driver and her three-year-old son.

After treatment for his cancer, Reuben returned home for a short while. The last time I saw him, he was sitting in his log house, peeling potatoes next to an oil-burning stove amidst a clutter of kitchen utensils, broken ladders, farming tools and old newspapers. He said he was sorry about his son's death but also relieved because Pancake in his drunkenness could no longer harm anyone. I still miss Reuben and although I have forgotten his face, I can clearly see the old man emerging from the woods to learn about the strangers who were building a cabin.

Now while sitting on my porch in January fog, I think about how the woods has shaped our lives over the last thirty-five years, how we have become a part of it, not merely living in it. We are in the rhythm of its seasons and feel close to the creatures who share it with us.

Offerings

The woods has offered me more than I could have imagined. It has taught about cycles, seasons, the passage of time, and has allowed me to translate its sights and sounds. It invited me to take a notebook to hollowed out places in the bluffs and write about melting snow, pictures in stone, acorns that look like wishbones, bones that look like twigs, wind in the trees, barking turkeys, coyote scat, the drumming of woodpeckers, curious kinglets and unidentified footsteps. It invited me to sit on a log by the South Fork and write about water tumbling over rocks, shadows of water striders, the patience of great blue herons, the choreography of cedar waxwings, the intimacy of spawning brook trout and how trout lilies got their name.

The Big Woods has given me birds. It has taught me how to identify them by sight and sound. When I moved here, I didn't know the difference between a downy and hairy woodpecker. Now, I can easily differentiate them, even at a distance. Likewise for chickadees and nuthatches. Vireo songs that once sounded alike are easy to tell apart and I no longer mistake the clicking notes of cardinals for juncos.

As an inhabitant of the woods, I have learned the habits and habitats of birds. This morning when I walked through my yard, down my driveway and along our township road, I passed the barberry bush where catbirds nest and the brushy opening where field sparrows build tiny grass cups and lay bluish white eggs with brown spots. I passed the tall basswood where blue-gray gnatcatchers use spider webs to weave grasses into a tiny cup and lichen to decorate the outside, the stump where chickadees take turns excavating beak-sized pieces of wood and the brush along the South Fork where a yellow warbler built a three story nest to avoid incubating eggs of the parasitic brown-headed cowbird. I thought about all the bald eagles and red-tailed hawks I've seen soaring over these familiar bluffs and the marsh where migrating sparrows and solitary sandpipers stop to rest before moving south or north.

The Big Woods has given me friendships through its invitation to birdwatchers who have come here to see our celebrities—tufted titmice at our feeders, pine grosbeaks in our cedars, a yellow-breasted chat in the field, a hooded warbler in a wooded ravine and the tropical spring festival of Baltimore orioles, scarlet tanagers, rose-breasted grosbeaks and indigo buntings.

Trout Lily

Over the years, the woods has changed and stayed the same. My neighborhood has seen the building of houses, barns, workshops and sheds. People continue to plant and harvest gardens, gather and burn firewood, plow snow and mow lawns. Some neighbors have left and others have moved in. The birds sing the same songs, but they are different birds. Generations of trout have come and gone, but their colors haven't changed. The order of seasons never varies. Trees are bare every winter. Leaves turn green every spring. Yet, no winter or spring is exactly like another. The Big Woods is always familiar, yet wind, sun, flood, drought, growth and decay ensure constant change.

I have changed. I have crows' feet now and I found a gray hair the other day. But, I still roam the woods and visit with the neighbors whose lives have touched mine.

A Man of History

We find him sitting at the entrance to his open garage in Lanesboro intent on caning a chair. Butterflies flutter around his head, but he seems not to have noticed them. He says he has been buying old chairs and repairing the caning in them for about twenty years. This hobby dovetails with Don Ward's interest in anything old, particularly regarding Lanesboro.

One day last year, Don appeared at my house in the Big Woods to talk about Dr. Johan Hvoslef, Lanesboro physician and naturalist at the turn of the last century. When Don had learned that I was transcribing some of the doctor's diaries, he gathered old newspaper articles featuring Dr. Hvoslef and brought them to me. He also invited me to visit him at his home where he has thousands of historical documents and artifacts.

Today, I have finally taken him up on that invitation. I have come with my artist friend Dana Gardner, who is here from his home in Berkeley for a six week visit. When Dana was growing up, the Gardners and the Wards were neighbors and good friends. Having Dana with me is a good way to break the ice.

Don invites us into his office/museum in the basement of his house where we find cabinets and shelves containing old books, fire maps and artifacts, such as jugs, bottles, glasses and toys. To our left is another room, which contains a desk, an old manual typewriter, a modern copy machine and shelves from floor to ceiling that hold loose-leaf binders with labels such as "Churches," "Bird's Eye Views," "Construction," "Disasters" and "Homes."

Monarch Butterfly

Don says he has been interested in local history as long as he can remember. He has lived in Lanesboro most of his life and his family has deep roots in the area. He was born in 1919 and spent his first three years on a farm in Amherst township, after which he moved with his family to Lanesboro. He graduated from Lanesboro High School in 1938, then worked in his dad's construction business before going to college to study civil engineering under a program offered by the Army.

In 1941, after only one year of college, as the United States entered World War II, Don was called to active duty. He spent most of the War in the Army Core of Engineers in England and France, where he helped to build airfields.

His interest in local history heightened when he returned to Lanesboro in 1945 after the war. He then began to build a network of like-minded people with whom he could swap old newspapers, pictures and artifacts. To this day, if he finds something of historical interest to someone in another part of the state, he sends it on. Frequently, he receives something in return.

In 1979, Don and his wife Alene opened an antique store in the Lanesboro building where Matt Bue, a professional photographer, once had his studio. When they took the building over, Don and Alene came into possession of many old photographs, which further sparked their interest in local history.

As we visit, one subject leads to another. Don talks about the Phoenix, a three-story hotel in Lanesboro that burned to the ground in 1885. The fire ignited, the story goes, from a still smoldering cigar butt that someone inadvertently flipped through an open window.

Lanesboro not only supported a grand hotel; it also at times supported up to four doctors, one of whom was Dr. Hvoslef, who died in 1920, a year after Don was born. I ask if he knows anything about a Dr. Drake who was a colleague of Hvoslef. Don says, "He delivered me."

Hvoslef spent much of his life collecting and cataloging natural artifacts and recording all the plants, insects, birds and other wildlife he observed. He kept meticulous records of his observations of nature just as Don keeps records of the history of human nature.

Don says such record keeping is not without its difficulties. The organization, which reflects the complexity of life itself, is never perfect. He says he's going to have to live to 104 to get everything done.

Dana and I finally leave, promising to come back another day. As we back out of his driveway, we wave to the Lanesboro historian who is again intent on caning a chair and oblivious to the butterflies hovering around him.

Abby's World

The Lanesboro library was our first stop. She found the children's section immediately and picked out a book with an elephant on the front cover sitting in a bathtub drinking tea. She sat in one of the small chairs and began to turn the pages. I picked out several more books for her, all of which she firmly discarded except for one with a big green frog on the cover. When we left she said, "Thank you, Nancy Bee, for taking me to this library."

Once outside, we decided to walk around the pond in Sylvan Park. I pointed out the geese swimming towards us. She thought they were coming to kiss her. We passed a woman walking with her little girl. Abby greeted the little girl enthusiastically and the two of them waved to each other repeatedly, as they walked around the pond in opposite directions.

Abby is my three-year-old great niece. She was to be with me all day. Because it was no more than a day, I had the luxury of giving her my complete attention and energy.

The park playground was a big hit. Abby immediately climbed the steps to the slides and slid down every one. She ran fearlessly back and forth across the swinging bridge. She was in a world that was exactly the right size, a world that I could see through her eyes, but one in which I felt like a giant.

Soon, a swarm of first graders came running out of the nearby school, shouting and laughing as though experiencing freedom for the first time. Abby joined the kids without hesitation. They did not seem to mind the small intruder as they made way for her and showed her how to use some of the equipment.

I let her play until she wore herself out. When we finally sat down on a bench, she said it was "refreshing" to rest because she was "all tuckered out." While sitting there, we looked at the pictures in the elephant book and made up our own stories to go with them.

Mourning Cloak Butterfly

Because I hadn't seen her for awhile, I was a little worried that Abby would be shy of me and afraid to leave the care of her grandmother, but she showed no shyness at all. However, on our way to my house in the woods she said that my husband, her Uncle Art, should use his high voice with her and then she wouldn't be afraid of him.

When she first saw Art, she clung to my leg and hid behind it, but her shyness didn't last long. Soon the three of us were playing ball and chasing butterflies. Little things, such as acorns and their caps, caterpillars, small spiders, autumn-colored leaves and butterflies, captured most of her attention. I realized that my interest in the small details of nature is one of the things that brings me close to children.

Everything was exciting to Abby, even a simple walk with Art and me each holding a hand and swinging her between us from time to time. "Swing me," she said. "Do it again." Every once in awhile, she stopped to pick up a present for her daddy or mommy—a leaf, a stick, a stone. Everything about our niece seemed beautiful and sweet to us right down to her little jeans and tee-shirt.

Finally, Abby and I settled down on the couch to watch a movie about Barney the dinosaur and one about Peter Rabbit. Her little body cuddled next to mine, the animation in her eyes and the expressiveness of her words seemed like miracles.

All too soon, it was time to take our niece back to her grandparent's house in Lanesboro where she babbled about the library, the playground, the kids, the acorns and their hats, Barney and the books about the frog and the elephant in the bathtub drinking tea.

My Favorite Places

I am here for the third time this year, but the first time alone. The trail through the narrow valley of Shattuck Creek, about five miles from my home, leads me deep into the forest. I look up at the big hardwood trees and down at a carpet of wildflowers.

The deeper I go, the more birds I hear. By their frantic behavior, I realize I have come uncomfortably close to nests of a rose-breasted grosbeak, indigo bunting and eastern towhee (our largest sparrow). Although I'm trying not to disturb them, the birds, unused to human traffic, see me as an intruder. I don't belong here as I do in my own part of the Big Woods where the birds are used to my presence.

A few years ago, this almost pristine area suffered the roar and ruts of off road vehicles. Now closed to motorized vehicles, its old wounds are healing and wild visitors are again becoming residents.

The habitat is right for the Acadian flycatcher, a rare bird in these parts and one whose population is declining due to habitat loss. I hope to hear one today, but I've been so engrossed in other sights and sounds that I have forgotten to listen for it. Suddenly, I hear its loud emphatic call. Was it real or my imagination? It calls again and now I am sure.

Another bird I hope to hear is a veery, a deep woods thrush that likes narrow wooded valleys like this one. The description of its song as sounding like a thumb running down the lines of a comb does not do it justice. Suddenly, I hear it. The bird is close, but I cannot see it in the dense foliage.

My first visit here this year was with my husband to see amethyst shooting stars among rock outcroppings along the township road just before the trail. My friend, Lori Slindee, from Harmony, had told me about these flowers. This was soon after she had invited me to join her garden club on its spring wildflower walk at the Hvoslef Wildlife Management Area, one of my favorite places and only a few miles from my home. There we spent a morning hiking in the bluffs where we found more than thirty species of spring flowers including trout-lilies, hepatica, rue-anemones, false rue-anemones, Dutchman's-breeches and violets. That morning, I learned that perennial wildflowers may grow underground for years before blooming, for example, fifteen years for the lady's slipper!

My second trip to Shattuck Creek was in the company of a man I barely knew, a man whose great knowledge about birds, wildflowers and all other things wild would have intimidated me but for his gentleness and lack of guile. I learned much from Craig that day, but he made it seem like we were learning from each other. Perhaps we were. The shooting stars were still blooming. Craig said they reminded him of his childhood home in Ohio where they were abundant.

When I reach my own woods again, familiarity makes it seem less magical than Shattuck Creek, but then it assumes a certain majesty when I think of how I saw it recently through visitors' eyes. My visitors were participants in the Elder Learning Institute Bird Class through the University of

Minnesota. The group had been to my house twice before. I enjoyed seeing some of the same people again and some new ones as well.

Amethyst Shooting Star

Every bird, common or not, interested my visitors. They were excited about the appearance of an indigo bunting, a tiny American redstart and a great crested flycatcher singing his maniacal song. Birds at the feeders, including goldfinch, nuthatches, chickadees, woodpeckers, hummingbirds and rose-breasted grosbeaks also drew attention. We flushed a catbird off her nest and looked at her four beautiful blue eggs. We looked deep into the woods at the storybook green of the forest floor glowing with purple geraniums.

I am grateful that these, my three favorite places in the Big Woods, still have the ability to entrance and amaze me, to welcome me as a familiar presence and to tolerate me as a stranger.

The Tortoise and the Hare

One can learn a lot about a marriage by watching how a couple works together.

Art and I just finished gathering our winter supply of firewood. At the beginning, we were nervous about our cranky backs because every part of the process, from cutting trees to stacking the wood, involves backbreaking labor. Once started, though, we ignored the pain, the sweat dripping into our eyes, even the bee stings.

We planned to cut medium sized trees around the periphery of a field adjacent to our house to make more room for grassland birds and wildflowers, like the yellow coneflowers that had just finished blooming there. We knew better than to cut big heavy trees deep in the woods as we had done in our younger years.

Deciding which trees to cut was harder than expected. When we saw sapsucker holes in neat little rows, we felt sad about depriving the sapsucker of its nectar. When we saw dead branches reaching into the sky, we felt sad about depriving hawks of their perches. Some trees were old friends. At one time, we didn't worry about these things, but over the years, we have become increasingly sensitive to the needs of other woodlanders.

In felling a tree, the first step was to cut a pie-shaped chunk from one side to insure that it would fall in the right direction. The next step was to cut on the opposite side until the tree came down. I watched as Art cut the first tree. Clearly, his skill had improved over the years. The chainsaw wasn't stuck and the tree fell as planned.

Coneflower

Next, he cut the smaller branches while I hauled them away. This was the part where Art used to criticize me for not hauling the branches fast enough or in the right direction. It felt like he not only didn't appreciate all the work I was doing, but that he also expected me to read his mind.

We have both changed over the years. This year I found that I could almost read my husband's mind if I paid close attention. I decided to let him be the boss since he has more skill in this area than I do. For his part, although he sometimes seemed exasperated with me, a new patience was also apparent.

The next step was to make stove length cuts in the trunk and larger branches. When Art finished the upper cuts, I rolled the logs over and held them in place so he could finish the job. Then, I busied myself throwing the wood into the wagon until he required my assistance again.

When the wagon was full, Art pulled it to the log splitter by the woodshed. We lifted the larger sizes of wood together and placed them on the splitter. As the pieces came off the splitter, we threw them on a pile along with the smaller pieces.

We didn't need words for these maneuvers. Our ability to coordinate our tasks while anticipating each other's needs felt good.

When it came time to stack the wood, we tried to do it together, but our work styles finally collided. I like to work slowly, methodically placing each log in just the right place, and not resting until I complete the job. Art's style is to work fast, rest, and then work fast again. I am the tortoise; he is the hare. He soon left the stacking to me and went to push the leftover brush to the periphery of our yard.

Although we can sometimes work as one, it is apparent that we are still individuals with our own styles. Over the years, without realizing when it began to happen, we have learned to compromise when it matters and when it doesn't, we work and play according to our separate personalities.

We worked for five days. At the end of each workday, we sat silently on the porch listening to the birdsong that replaced the sounds of the chainsaw, tractor and log splitter.

Our yard looks different now. The cutting of trees has changed the play of light and shadow. The birds, squirrels and chipmunks forage in the new piles of brush. When we look out our kitchen window at our well-stocked woodshed, we see more than a supply of fuel for the winter; we see a history of our life together.

A Rich Inheritance

I have been grieving over the loss of a dear friend, Johan C. Hvoslef, who died in 1920, but who died for me only a few days ago.

In 1876, after emigrating from Norway and attending medical school in Chicago, Hvoslef arrived in Lanesboro where he practiced medicine and observed nature for forty-four years. From 1881-1918, he filled fifty-six notebooks, the first thirty-eight in Norwegian, the last eighteen in English, with accounts of his daily activities, world events, the weather, birds and plants.

I have just completed transcription of the journals written in English. After being with Dr. Hvoslef for three years, I am reluctant to let him go and will continue as consultant to the translator of the Norwegian diaries whose work will soon begin.

Funding for this work has come through the office of Carrol Henderson, Minnesota Department of Natural Resources Nongame Supervisor. He wrote,

Dr. Hvoslef has left us with a remarkable record of over 40 years of diaries with natural history, weather and wildlife records... Because of the significant amount of information on nongame wildlife species present in these records, I wish to indicate my interest in and support of efforts to get these records transcribed and subsequently published. As far as I can tell, Fillmore County has the best historical record of wildlife present in the pioneer settlement era of any county in Minnesota because of these Hvoslef journals.

The notebooks offer a unique opportunity to compare the natural and human history of Hvoslef's time with that of the present. They also offer an intimate view of a private and melancholy man who probably confided more in his diaries than he did in any person and whose social contacts were limited to casual encounters and a prolific correspondence with other scientists.

A great part of Hvoslef's observations took place on his daily walks to the Lanesboro cemetery, which began in 1898 with the death of his six-year-old daughter Agnes, an only child born late in the lives of the doctor and his wife. Before his daughter's death, Hvoslef frequently watched birds from his boathouse on Mill Pond Lake behind the Lanesboro dam. Since that time, due to silting, the lake, now called Lost Lake, and its variety of species have disappeared.

He also made observations on trips to see patients, which often took him to the uplands around Lanesboro where one could still see virgin prairies. There he found pasqueflowers, prairie smoke, leadplant, wild indigo, prairie clovers and downy gentian. Sometimes he traveled near Amherst and the wildlife management area that now carries his name, "up through those very remarkable ravines where the cliffs were covered with the flowering beautiful *Dodecatheon media* [shooting stars]." (May 20, 1910)

Although he was a man of science, the doctor was also gentle and emotionally responsive to the natural world. "Three *Colinus virginianus* [northern bobwhite] in the dreadful cold among the mountain-like snowdrifts... How I wished I had had some food to throw out to them!" (January 15, 1912)

He was an avid reader of local, national and international publications. He collected maps from around the world and drew maps of his paths through fields and woods.

Northern Bobwhites in Snow

Hvoslef often predicted and wrote about storms, floods and fires. In his time, Lanesboro had its share of all three, especially fires. The grand Phoenix Hotel burned in 1885. Over time, fire destroyed all the mills on Mill Pond Lake. In 1917, a fire on Church Hill destroyed the Lutheran Church, the high school and the old stone school. This incident led the doctor to speculate that the fire, which occurred during World War I, was the result of a German plot.

My work has allowed me to know the inner workings of this complicated and interesting man who has told me more than I ever expected to learn about the natural history of Fillmore County one hundred years ago and with whom I share an enduring love of wildflowers and birds.

Although the diaries remind us sadly of the natural diversity we have lost, perhaps they will also serve as inspiration to preserve and improve what we still have.

Truth and Reconciliation

A discussion about truth and reconciliation in South Africa was playing on Minnesota Public Radio last Sunday as I approached Faribault, the town of my childhood and youth. I was on my way to the ninetieth birthday party for Ray Freund, a dear family friend and the only friend who remained loyal to my dad until the end.

On the radio, I listened as a woman reporter talked about Eugene de Kock, the man called "Prime Evil" for his relentless pursuit and extermination of anti-apartheid activists. She told of the widows who forgave him when he faced them and confessed to killing their husbands. She visited de Kock herself and came to believe in his contrition. In a moment of pity, she touched his hand and the broken man cried.

I began to cry when I entered Faribault through my old neighborhood on the East Side. I wondered if the program on the radio had anything to do with my tears. Were there old wrongs for which I needed forgiveness, such as being inattentive to my little sister, having parties with questionable characters when my parents were gone, exacting revenge on a former friend, and, above all, being impatient with my dad? In those years before his suicide, I felt pity and took care of my dad, but obviously not well enough. Possibly, there were people I needed to forgive, such as the kids who teased me for being tall, the boys who didn't ask me to dance and the obsessive father whose negativity affected my worldview.

Maybe my tears had nothing to do with truth and reconciliation. Maybe they only represented sentiment.

I was early for the party so I drove around the East Side. Someone had put an addition on my old house. My dad's crimson king maples in the front yard were still there, not much taller, but with huge gnarly old trunks. At the house where a cruel and sadistic kid once lived, I saw a woman tending flowers in a yard full of flowers, a world onto itself. I drove past the house where Ray has lived for more than fifty years.

As I approached the Knights of Columbus Hall, the place of Ray's party, I felt that old familiar shyness that has played such a big role in my life. Would I recognize anyone other than Ray? Would I stand there awkwardly trying to blend in? Why did I come? I kept driving and suddenly found myself in front of the house where I spent my first five years. Memory is a funny thing. I've looked for that house other times in the past without being able to find it.

Finally, I summoned the courage to enter the party. Although I hadn't seen them for years, I immediately recognized Ray's boys. They looked just like their father. I had forgotten what Ray's wife looked like, but remembered when I saw his daughter Mary Jo. Ray seemed so happy to see me that I knew I had been right to come.

Other than the Freunds, I talked with a man who hugged me and said that my dad was the best teacher he had ever had; a former classmate who lives with his mother and sells antiques on E-bay; our old next-door neighbor who said that the East Side is full of young families now, like we were in the 1940s and 50s. These families are the future, I thought, and suddenly felt irrelevant and old. Having no one else to talk with, I left as gracefully as I could.

White-throated Sparrow

I was happy to be driving home. When I reached Fillmore County, I began to feel younger and more relevant than I felt in Faribault. I belong here, I thought, because I have been active in this community through my writing and as an advocate for the environment. I don't feel so shy here. When I see people I know, I don't always cross the street or hide behind a tree to avoid them. When I finally drove up my driveway and heard the evening chorus of white-throated sparrows singing the sweet partial songs we hear in fall, I knew I was back where I needed to be.

Perhaps the conflicts of childhood are impossible to resolve. Perhaps the best we can do is make peace with the past and count that as reconciliation enough.

Old Haunts

R ed-bellied woodpeckers, chickadees and nuthatches, but no migratory birds, were present on the edge of my woods one fall when I found my way onto an old tractor trail that leads down to the South Fork of the Root River. When I reached a certain big maple, I noted how much it has grown since I first saw it in 1972 on the day Art and I had known, without saying a word, that we had decided to buy this patch of woods.

Ownership is important, I thought, as I worked my way down the trail. I can sit here on any log I want. I can hug a tree without embarrassment. No one will bother me. My introversion will cause neither me nor anyone else discomfort. Suddenly, a ruffed grouse exploding from the brush interrupted my thoughts. The smell of damp earth reached my nostrils. The creek became audible. You can't turn inward here, I thought. Introversion is impossible in this place that enlivens the senses and demands attention.

The little wetland at the bottom of the bluff looked much as it always had. I used to spend hours watching water striders skipping across its surface and song sparrows singing on its edges. It was good to visit the wetland again, something I seldom do now that my aging body imposes restrictions. Ignoring my old muscles, I acted as though I was young and able to wander the bottomlands all day long. I used to come here often to gain perspective on the thorny problems of my life. Age has its compensations, I thought. My problems are still thorny, but I am mellower now and no longer experience them with such anxiety.

Drawing 1 Wood Duck

I wound my way through the brittle fall vegetation to the creek. A trout blurred past on its way upstream. A winter wren fussed among the rocks on the opposite bank. A late great blue heron rose on its powerful wings and a single wood duck floated in the water. I passed the big pool where we used to go skinny-dipping and found the old cottonwood with its exposed roots that crawl over rocks before digging into the earth.

The bluff rose in front of me. My old path was still visible, but its difficult footing made me consider going back the way I had come. I decided to risk it and soon found myself scrambling up the bluff on hands and knees until I finally reached some familiar patches of yew and surer footing. High chickadee-like notes alerted me to a golden-crowned kinglet foraging in the yew.

Following scars left from long ago cattle, I came to the creek again then began working my way up once more. A blue jay screeched nearby and a pileated woodpecker called in the distance. Signs of my early presence appeared in the stubby ends of red cedar branches that I had cut long before. I followed these signs until the slope became more gradual and the understory was open. I saw that the mature oaks and maples here had given birth to new generations.

Looming across my northern fence line was the giant unfinished house that my off-road vehicle loving neighbor has been building for two years. Suddenly, I envisioned a line of houses all along the bluff. Ownership is important, I thought. I can keep this vision from becoming reality. I can preserve this land so that even when I am gone, the trees will continue to grow and the birds will continue to nest and find food here. Or can I? How can I protect it from pollution? How can I protect it from global warming? Will my sixty-two acres of woods provide sufficient habitat while urban sprawl increasingly fragments the forest surrounding it?

I had just witnessed the poorest fall migration of the last twenty years here in the Big Woods. I knew that breeding failures resulting from our cold damp summer were partly to blame. Migratory songbirds, however, have been declining for the past sixty years. Due to low numbers, some species may not be able to recover from the lack of young birds to maintain populations. I thought ahead to spring with hope and dread. Will I see the warblers again only one at a time instead of the waves I once saw? Will the sparrows arrive on time, come earlier because of global warming, or not come at all?

Reluctant to separate from the wild world, I stood still, absorbing it with all my senses before returning to my house and everyday life.

Adventure in the Big Woods

The day was mine to give. We hadn't seen each other in two years and in that time the little boy had become a teenager hinting at a man. I remembered the days when we made swords out of sticks, searched for snails and fossils and hiked through Shattuck Creek. I planned the day carefully, but worried that a picnic lunch and exploring the bluffs wouldn't measure up to expectations he had of his old aunt who had created those memorable days of the past.

When I arrived at his grandparents' house in Lanesboro where he was visiting from his home in a distant state, he seemed reluctant to leave. During our drive to my house in the Big Woods, he didn't say much. After preparing our picnic lunch, we walked down the road to the animal trail that leads into the bluffs.

A short way up the trail, I heard a twittering sound and saw a bird zooming through the undergrowth. I called out, "It's a woodcock! The first one this spring." My nephew exclaimed, "How did you know that? I hardly saw it." I explained that I had been expecting to see this bird, the habitat was right, I recognized its sound and saw a flash of orange feathers. He asked if there were such things as "birdologists." I told him they're called ornithologists.

"Look at those cliffs," Kevin said. "I'll bet we could find caves in them where someone could live." In his enthusiasm and conjectures, he reminded me of another nephew, his father David, with whom I used to have similar adventures. I intended to let Kevin explore as he wished but first we went to an open rock-strewn area to eat our lunch. He was full of questions, wondering if Native Americans had ever been there, what it was like before the white man came, and if a person could make money by knowing about nature.

I realized in his companionship that I was sometimes lonely up in these bluffs, in spite of the fact that there was no one I wanted to take with me. I feared the presence of another person would take the magic out of the experience. But I was willing to do it for my nephew and found, to my delight, that my young companion enhanced the magic. He was giving the day to me as much as I was giving it to him.

After lunch, we hiked to the top of the bluffs. Up and down, we climbed. In a hollowed out place Kevin saw a snake with a yellow eye and dared me to crawl in to see if it was alive, which I did, only to find it was part of the rock. He walked on ledges where I didn't dare follow and wanted to climb on ledges that he could see were impossible. " My dad would go up there," he said. "He's not afraid of anything." He couldn't find a way down from one of the ledges, so I pushed on a small tree until he could reach it and he swung to the ground like Tarzan.

Finally, after slipping in mud, he was ready to leave and I feared he was no longer enjoying our day. But soon after we reached the township road, he eyed the spring fed stream that flows into the South Fork. "I'm a stream boy," he said, and was at the water's edge in a flash, constructing a spear to catch trout. Unmindful of the March cold, he was suddenly in the stream, throwing his spear and skipping stones.

Cold feet and pebbles in his shoes eventually convinced the stream boy that he'd had enough. I could see he was tired. I was too. Tired or not, when he eyed the culvert at the entrance to our driveway, he had to crawl down and walk through it, exclaiming at the echo his voice made. Back at my house, Kevin's energy rose again when Art showed him a new computer game. In the meantime, I washed his shoes and socks and wished for more such opportunities.

American Woodcock

Too soon, it was time to return Kevin to his grandparents' house. When I see my nephew again, his voice will be deeper and he will be more of a man. I hope his interests in nature will continue, but whatever happens, I believe he will always have fond memories of this day, as will I.

Lessons in Choreography

O h my! Oh my!" I exclaimed aloud as I stood on our township road near the South Fork bridge watching the blue-headed, black-faced bird, the first black-throated blue warbler ever recorded in Fillmore County. I watched until the stunning creature disappeared, then lamented that some of my best sightings occur when I am alone.

Three days later, on September 1, I joined my La Crosse birding partner Fred Lesher to look for warblers at Beaver Creek Valley State Park near Caledonia. As many as thirty-five species of these small, lively insect eaters with intricate colors and markings migrate through our area each spring and fall. Although we once saw up to twenty-five species in a day, numbers have dwindled in recent years, mostly due to habitat loss, and except for the black-throated blue that I saw in the Big Woods, neither Fred nor I had been having much luck.

When we arrived at Beaver Creek, we heard no birds singing. Silence also met us at the swinging footbridge, but part way down the trail, we heard squeaky notes and found an American redstart flashing orange and black plumage. Both of us are dedicated pessimists, not only about birds but about the state of the world, so the little redstart, a common species, didn't inspire much hope.

When we reached the first creek crossing, Fred, who is recovering from major back surgery, said he had to rest, but just then a fluttering movement caught our eyes and soon a yellowish bird with a black eyeline appeared, a Tennessee warbler. Still with little hope, but forgetting about resting, we searched the trees, simultaneously focusing on the same falling leaves and then, to our pleasure, on a black-and-white warbler, whose stylish markings make up for its lack of color.

Blackburnian Warbler

At the second crossing, birds numerous as bugs flew high in the trees, dropped down like leaves, wove among branches and maneuvered around each other. Our pessimism turned into optimism as we watched and listened with binoculars partly raised, turning this way and that, looking up, looking down, two steps forward, two steps back in an effort to determine each species. An onlooker might have wondered about the strange couple dancing in the woods. The state of the world and the aches of our aging bodies melted away as we feasted our eyes on chestnut-sided, golden-winged, blue-winged, magnolia, black-throated green and Blackburnian warblers, all wearing plumage only slightly less brilliant than in spring. Too soon, the wave of migrants moved on. We looked at our watches. The morning had disappeared.

On September 4, my husband and I joined our friend Dennis Carter and other Iowa birders on their annual Labor Day outing to Cardinal Marsh near Cresco and, this year, to Twin Springs in Decorah as well. The marsh offered us good looks at delicate shorebirds, cryptically-plumaged sora rails, hundreds of swooping swallows, a couple of bugling sandhill cranes, a few vireos and a few warblers, but the highlight of our outing was at Twin Springs where we experienced waves of birds such as we might never see again. Craning our necks, running from spot to spot, maneuvering around each other almost as skillfully as the warblers, we focused our binoculars on a black-throated green partially hidden behind a leaf, the bright yellow belly of a Nashville foraging in the brush, a black-and white imitating a nuthatch, a bay-breasted sporting just a touch of its rich rufous breeding plumage and multiple numbers of nine other species.

After each of these outings, I tried to articulate why warblers have such a hold on me. Intellectually, I enjoy the challenges of identification. I admire the little creatures because of their ability to survive long flights to Central or South America, because they know what I can never know and because they fit their niches perfectly in the age-old web of migration, while I often feel like I don't fit anywhere. But their emotional hold on me has little to do with intellect, nothing to do with words. It's about a moment in time, witnessing the physical presence of these birds in their natural habitats, their amazing colors and wings, their songs, their eyes, spindly legs and feet. It's about the warbler dance.

The Road not Taken

One day in October, I walked deep into my woods where the paths we created more than two decades ago haven't been maintained. I took a wrong turn and that made all the difference in how I saw the woods. There were changes of course. The prickly ash, which we once so carefully trimmed, reached across paths tearing at clothes and skin. The deer and other creatures who helped maintain our paths, had created new ones because of fallen trees, thus making me more disoriented than I might have been.

I passed some trees that looked familiar, but they seemed to be in the wrong places. A red-bellied woodpecker called, making me feel at home in spite of being lost. I came to one of the benches we had placed along our paths. It wasn't where I expected it to be. My brain tried to make it right and failed. Wasn't this where I used to see a winter wren foraging near the ground?

Although I didn't know where I had gone wrong, it soon became obvious that I was going down toward the South Fork instead of toward our southern fence line as I intended. So I gave up on the paths and headed in the opposite direction.

Goldenrod seeds in a brushy area fell off onto my clothes as I pushed through. A chipmunk, with bulging pouches, scurried by. Another startled me with its alarm call. I heard a flock of robins and thought maybe they were eating red cedar berries in the spot where, long ago, I had found a flock of pine grosbeaks.

Eastern Chipmunk

I saw the big oaks as if for the first time and the black cherry trees were larger and more numerous than I remembered. Finally, I came to an old gnarly maple, unmistakable due to a branch we had cut for firewood and later regretted. I sat on a bench there where I used to watch red-tailed hawks, bald eagles and vultures soaring overhead. A chickadee came close, but no raptors flew over.

Our fence line and the field on the other side were only about fifty yards away. I used to walk across this field to an old tractor path high in the bluffs amidst towering white pines where I crawled out to a slender point overlooking the creek. From there I could watch fishermen casting their lines for trout and look across the valley to the old Simley farm and what is now the Hvoslef Wildlife Management Area. Once, I watched a red-tailed hawk feeding her young in a nest just below my perch.

As I approached the field, I saw a cabin where no building had ever been. I circled it like a wild animal. I could almost feel myself sniffing for danger. No one was there, so I cautiously stepped onto the porch and looked in a window. I had to shade my eyes because the sun was reflecting the field making it difficult to see inside. I saw stairs leading to a loft and a stovepipe hanging partway down from the ceiling. The cabin was empty except for something lying on the floor. I caught my breath when I saw the long bill of what looked like a dead woodcock. When I went to the back of the cabin and looked in another window, I realized the woodcock was a toy.

I returned home the way I intended to come. Although fallen trees blocked the path at several places, I found my way easily enough. Everything came into focus. I crossed the ravine where, one spring, I found a ruffed grouse nest and heard a hooded warbler singing his spring song. I finally reached the bench I had been looking for and while resting there, I watched a winter wren foraging near the ground.

Winter Wandering

The old fear of missing a bus or train, or not exiting at the right stop, added a touch of adventure to the ride. Art and I had driven to a parking lot near Fort Snelling from where we caught the light rail into downtown Minneapolis. The ride, powered by electricity, was quiet and smooth as we glided past the Veterans' Hospital, Minnehaha Park, Lake Street and other familiar places. Our exit was the Warehouse District, the last station on the line.

Memories returned of bus trips to downtown Minneapolis when I was in college and all the people I met who seemed exotic to the small town girl that I was. Visions came to mind of bus, train and subway rides in other cities—San Francisco, New York, Chicago, Rome, Amsterdam, Stockholm and one winter Sunday when I waited for a bus in Cologne, wishing I had worn warm boots. A bus came, but didn't stop. I finally went to a restaurant to warm my feet. I ordered tea and, feeling faint, put my head on the table until the waitress said I could not sleep there. My German wasn't adequate to explain what was wrong, so I drank my tea and left. Fortunately, I quickly caught a bus.

After leaving the train, Art and I wandered down Hennepin Avenue. He, the former street-wise city kid, pointed to the top of the Lumber Exchange building where he and his friends used to loiter. I reminded him of 1971, when we returned to Minneapolis from Arizona with no money in our pockets. The first job I found was at a health food store on LaSalle Avenue. I took a bus to work and afterwards sometimes shopped for groceries nearby on Hennepin Avenue at the Great Northern Market, which no longer exists. I added the price of each item as I shopped to make sure I had enough money to pay the bill. Then I walked down the avenue to Bridgeman's, where I waited for the bus to go home. Bridgeman's too is now gone.

Blue Jay Screeching

Art and I turned off Hennepin and headed towards Nicollet Avenue. He pointed to a building where his older sister used to work. She took him out for lunch when he visited her there. We both remembered eating at the Forum, a cafeteria on Seventh Street between Hennepin and Nicollet Avenues. The Forum no longer exists, but we soon found a Chinese restaurant, where we had lunch.

After lunch, a walk down Nicollet Avenue took us to where Dayton's, now Macy's, once was. We entered Macy's through a familiar door and soon found the layout hasn't changed much since it was Dayton's. In fact, the Oval Room is still there, by the same name. I remembered passing it with my sister and mom on our yearly trips to buy school clothes. Art and I found good sales in the Oval Room, such as a jacket that was half-price, only $900.00.

Outside again, we felt the cold, windy winter weather. Few people were on the streets and we wondered if shoppers were at the malls instead. A number of buildings were empty and had for rent or lease signs on them. When we returned inside to wander the skyways, we found the shopping crowd.

While resting on a bench at the inside court of the IDS building, we watched a man arranging his belongings in a grocery cart, several women reading books and teens sauntering through in baggy clothes. Our tired old legs told us our day was winding down and it was time to catch the light rail again. Back on the train, we glided past those familiar places to the parking lot where we found our car and began our drive home to the Big Woods.

Our trip to Minneapolis, I soon realized, had stripped me of my winter weariness. I began noticing the details of the world around me with greater enthusiasm, the blue jay screeching just above my head, the red-tailed hawk escaping a gang of crows, tiny bones in a patch of bare earth.

Stalking

In his *Field Guide to Nature Observation and Tracking*, Tom Brown gave directions for stalking silently: touch outside ball of foot down first, roll to the inside, then heel down, toes down, apply weight, glide forward. With practice, I learned to move silently even in dry leaves, but too slowly to be practical.

Brown also wrote about stationary stalking: select a place, wait, muscles relaxed, senses alert, mind open to the wild. One morning, following his instructions, I sat on a bench in our woods, feeling like I was part of the woods; I belonged there. Soon, a deer and her fawn came near. I barely breathed. I noted the dark outline of their ears and the lighter fur inside. While the mother watched, the baby came close enough to touch, sniffed and looked, then walked back to its mom and they slowly moved off together.

Author Annie Dillard wrote about stalking muskrats along Tinker Creek in Virginia's Blue Ridge Mountains where she lived. She usually waited on a particular footbridge and when she saw ripples in the water, remained absolutely still, sometimes in awkward positions. She saw muskrats then, but one small move and they were gone.

My actions were almost the same, but I waited under a particular tree near my home along the South Fork. Once, a muskrat climbed out of the water and sat hunched up on a rock grooming itself. Suddenly it froze and I feared it had discovered me, but it was looking at a mink slinking over rocks. The muskrat slipped into the water. The mink continued on its way. Later, I learned that minks are the primary predators of muskrat young.

On a sunny morning a few days later, I sat on the bank of Blagsvedt Run, which flows into the South Fork. I looked into a pool of clear water and saw reflections of the sun and fallen branches. A water strider skimmed across the pool. When I looked into the water again, six fish, each about a foot long, materialized before my eyes. Had they been there all along? They were mostly green with red dots, had reddish bellies and red fins with white edges. Later, I identified the fish as brook trout, the only native trout species in Minnesota.

Brook Trout

I visited the brookies many times and one fall morning discovered a female sweeping stones into a redd (nest) with her tail while a male in fine breeding garb showing a bright red belly hovered just ahead. Suddenly, he flew into the air, circled back, wove his body around hers, then hovered again. Finally they swam in parallel, mouths open, bodies arched, breathing fast; they quivered for a moment, neither touching the other. Then he sped away while she remained sweeping across her redd.

Stalking is a solo activity for me as is writing about the natural world, but they evolved with the help of other naturalists and writers, like Annie Dillard and Tom Brown to whom I will always be grateful.

It's Only a Building

When I sorted my mom's clothes after her death, I found a pair of knit pants that still held her shape. A tissue in a pocket held the ineffable mother-scent only a child can recognize. After my father died, I spent many days in my parent's house going through their belongings. I slept in their bed, sinking my hip into the indentations from their hips. My mom's knitting needles, entwined with a half-finished sweater, still sat in the wooden bowl where she had left them six years earlier. My dad's soap-on-a-rope still hung in the shower. I had to remind myself that the house and its contents were only inanimate objects, merely human artifacts.

My computer now rests on the walnut desk my dad built more than fifty years ago. When I sit here writing, I sometimes recall my mom at this desk composing her Sunday letter to my grandma. The scene is different now. I look through windows deep into the Big Woods and check to see if the barred owl is perching in his favorite basswood tree. I remember my husband building these windows. I remember painting the molding around them. When I stand up to stretch and wander into the kitchen, I note the cupboards my dad built and remember the day he installed them.

Barred Owl in Basswood

The life of our house mixes with our history in the Big Woods. It brings back memories of the rainy day during which we dug holes for the posts that would be the foundation and the sucking sounds our feet made when we dragged them up out of the mud and the indigo bunting that kept us company with its song that sounded like "Fire! Fire! Where? Where? Here. Here." It brings back memories of the Amherst Township supervisors who visited while we were shingling the roof and who then decided that we were worthy of a culvert for our driveway. Like the shell of a turtle fits its back, our house has grown to fit our needs. To the one bedroom bungalow with two porches that we built in 1976, we later added two studies and another porch.

This house contains memories of birthday parties, nieces and nephews running up and down the hallways, Thanksgiving dinners, laughter, anger and reconciliation. It contains all my computer discs filled with poems, letters and manuscripts. It contains old fur and memories of six beloved cats who are no longer with us.

We thought we would live out our lives in this house but after almost thirty years we find our aging bodies are less inclined to cut the necessary firewood to keep us warm in winter, maintain our steep driveway and drive thirty miles roundtrip for groceries. We are preparing now for the next stage of our lives.

These days, I see our house differently, knowing that in a couple of years it will no longer exist. In the meantime, there is no reason to replace the old moss-covered shingles or the window cracked by a stone that the lawnmower threw at it, redo the wood floors scratched by chairs and claws, or finally finish the bathroom ceiling.

I like the idea that there will be little sign of human habitation left in this patch of the Big Woods when the DNR takes over our land as an addition to the Hvoslef Wildlife Management Area and demolishes our house. The house, after all, is only a building. It is not a sentient being. It has no personality, although my three cats may think it does. I have to admit, though, that a part of me wonders if she will feel pain with the ripping off of her roof and walls.

Living in a Dream

It is July 2008 and Preston, about fifteen miles from the Big Woods, is our home now. Our new house is bright and airy. Every window has a good view, something our cats quickly discovered. The large, private backyard has an herb garden, a vegetable garden and a flower garden. Around the house and along the edges of our property are day lilies, hostas, lilies-of-the-valley, bluebells, several young white pines, purple and white lilacs and other plantings I don't recognize. On two sides of us are large mature firtrees that belong to neighbors.

The sounds in Preston are not the same as country sounds. We hear lawnmowers, traffic, a jackhammer, birds we didn't hear in the woods and neighbors' voices. I've met some of my new neighbors, Julie, Mary, Stacy and Kevin, all friendly.

But my new town and house still don't seem like home. I feel like I'm living in a dream and will wake up and be back in the Big Woods and our house there won't be empty, our yard will be mowed and the birds will be coming to the feeders that have magically returned to their former places.

Taking time away from chores to walk in my new town is making me feel more at home here. I have walked down a trail that I can reach in ten minutes by foot. When other walkers see my binoculars, they ask questions about birds, which I am happy to answer. I met my neighbor Julie along the trail a couple times and we have talked about turkey vultures and great blue herons. Julie brought us rice crispy bars as a house-warming gift. I have walked to the bank, the grocery store and the farmers' market. I feel like a member of the community when people recognize me at these places and say hello.

Ruby-throated Hummingbird

Familiar furniture and the presence of our pets help to provide a sense of home as does working in my yard. I have planted tomatoes and lettuce, weeded the flowerbeds, dug up some dandelions and mowed the lawn. The bird feeders are drawing many grackles and starlings but also some other species such as red-bellied and hairy woodpeckers, an oriole pair, ruby-throated hummingbirds, catbirds, chickadees, nuthatches, mourning doves and a few goldfinch. I love sitting on our deck in the evenings and watching the flights of chimney swifts.

Soon I expect that I will no longer feel like I am living in a dream, but I wouldn't mind dreaming now and then of life in the Big Woods.

Change and Continuity

More than four years after our move to Preston, my house seems like home, that is most of the time. Once in awhile I feel the presence of its former owners and suddenly realize the colors of the rooms, the light fixtures, the stove, refrigerator, sinks, the arrangement of the rooms have nothing to do with decisions we made, unlike our Big Woods house that we designed and built ourselves. Our books, pictures and furniture seem to belong here, though, while still eliciting memories.

On this warm January day, not quite warm enough for sitting on our deck, I look out my kitchen windows and see a path to bird feeders and a heated birdbath where chickadees quickly grab a seed or take a quick drink and fly away while goldfinch, house finch, purple finch and pine siskins stop for longer periods of eating and drinking. Woodpeckers come for suet and blue jays zoom in scaring all the other birds. Squirrels forage for dropped seeds and look longingly at the feeders that they cannot reach. An opossum forages with the squirrels and deer saunter by at the edge of our yard.

This morning I walked to the post office and from there to the City Trail around town along the South Branch of the Root River. Didn't see many birds. Greeted some friendly dogs walking their humans. As I approached my house again, I heard barking and saw Teddy the beautiful little dog who lives across the street, greeting me though a window then appearing in another window where we greeted each other.

Ruffed Grouse

When no snow is on the ground, I walk other trails around town. My favorite is a wooded section of the Harmony / Preston Trail that I reach by road about three miles from home. One day while walking there, a sound reached my ears as of someone rustling through dry leaves. I turned and found a ruffed grouse foraging in the underbrush about five feet away. I thought about how I used to hear grouse drumming in the Big Woods and see them, especially when a startled one exploded from nearby brush as they often do. The grouse in front of me seemed to have no fear. It stepped closer, poking at leaves, turning them over, closer until it was about two feet away. It appeared healthy. I had time to study the shades in its feathers and look into its dark eyes. As I walked away, the strange bird followed me, or seemed to, for a short while.

70

Last fall, Art and I walked the same trail one late afternoon. When we reached the second footbridge, we stopped to look at a beaver den and saw a beaver carrying a mouth full of branches, another one grooming itself on the bank of Camp Creek and a third swimming under water. We stood as still as we could. Nevertheless, the beaver on the bank slipped into the creek and slapped its big flat tail in warning.

Every season of the year since moving to Preston, we have visited Forestville State Park, which is nearby. Last year during fall migration we found a picnic table there in a secluded area along the Root River where Art set up his equipment to take photos while I walked one of my favorite trails. Yellow-rumped warblers were thick as mosquitoes. White-throated sparrows scratched in the leaves as did fox sparrows and the first juncos of the season. I saw bald eagles, hermit thrushes, brown creepers, kinglets and rose-breasted grosbeaks. When I returned to the picnic table, I found Art sitting among many of the species I was ready to brag about seeing.

I still visit many of the places in Fillmore County I frequented while living in the woods—back country roads, the Hvoslef or Beaver Creek wildlife management areas, hidden places in the limestone bluffs, spring-fed streams like Shattuck Creek or Duschee Creek. I still follow the main lesson I learned in the Big Woods, which is noticing the details of the world around me. I have paid attention to how a stream rushes over rocks, slows down in deeper spots where sun shimmers on the water in shades of silver and a fish creates ripples from below, dimpling the water with widening circles that create moving shadows on overhanging branches. The limestone bluffs draw my attention to their formations, colors and caves. Sitting under overhanging bluffs, I look at the surrounding dirt and notice little ribs, vertebrae and skulls, indigestible bones left perhaps by coyotes.

In my backyard, as spring approaches I notice the first buds on the ash tree and the shrubs we've planted, the chives and garlic that poke out of the ground in March. I find myself poking in the dirt to make sure the perennial flowers are on their way up and when I find them, they seem like miracles. The most significant change for me since our move is my interest in vegetable and flower gardening, inspired by the gardens already here, and a willingness to give up some of my bird walks to plant, weed, or harvest.

While looking out my kitchen windows on this warm and foggy January day, I think about all that I have taken with me from the Big Woods, what has changed and what has stayed the same.

Acknowledgments

Thanks to Tom Driscoll, editor and author, for his faith in my ability to write another book. Thanks to Beadrin Youngdahl, friend and author, for her encouragement and advice. In appreciation for artist Dana Gardner, whose drawings have greatly enhanced this book, our fifth collaboration. In gratitude to my husband Art without whom I would not have had these stories to tell. And for their friendship and support, thanks to Ann Abrams, Jan Burns, Sue Carlson, Marilynn Ford, Susie Gysland, Mary Lewis and Marcia Neely. Some of the essays in this book are revised columns written between 1995-2011 for the *Fillmore County Journal* and *Minnesota Birding*.

About the Author

Nancy Overcott grew up in Faribault, Minnesota. She is the author of *Fifty Common Birds of the Upper Midwest*, and *Fifty Uncommon Birds of the Upper Midwest* (University of Iowa Press, 2006-2007), and an earlier volume, *At Home in the Big Woods* (Taxon Media, 2002).

About the Illustrator

Dana Gardner, Berkeley, California watercolor artist-illustrator, was born in Wisconsin. When he was seven, a kid with a love of birds and drawing, Dana and his family moved to Lanesboro. He has collaborated with Nancy Overcott on the three books listed above and has illustrated many field guides as well as bird books with other authors.

& Remember.

No matter your skill as an author, **Lost Lake Folk Art** will enable you to tell your story. We can help you with the writing if required through ghost, surrogate, project writing and complete editorial services. Your life, your farm, your family history or town history, your high school, senior class trip, championship season, the company you built or the one you quit, your first job, first love, honeymoon, the golden years, whatever it might be, it is never too late to capture those memories for others to treasure. Everyone has a story to tell. Let us help you tell yours.

Find more information at
contact@shipwrecktbooks.com
www.shipwrecktbooks.com
P.O. Box 20, Lanesboro, MN 55949

IN®
DIE

www.ingramcontent.com/pod-product-compliance
Lightning Source LLC
Chambersburg PA
CBHW081701270326
41933CB00017B/3235